Dear W
Paul

Barbara Grant
2004

Dear World: A Suicide Letter
Paul E. Jones

ZassCo., Inc.
5054 Western Hills Ave
Cincinnati, OH 45238
513.921.2403
sell1@iglou.com
www.TheInternetDepartment.com

ISBN: 1-55395-595-1
National Library of Canada Cataloguing in Publication Data

Jones, Paul E. (Paul Edward)
        Dear World: a Suicide Letter / Paul E. Jones
ISBN 1-55395-595-1
        1.   Manic-depressive persons. 2. Suicide. I Title.
RC515.J65 2003   616.89.5.0093   C2003-900245-4

Bulk rate discounted purchasing is
available by contacting the publishing
coordinator listed below.

Published and Distributed by:
ZassCo., Inc.
5054 Western Hills Ave.
Cincinnati, OH 45238
513.921.2403
www.bipolarbooks.com
sell1@iglou.com

Cover Design and Edited by:
Sue Veldkamp
Matschca Design, Inc.
Cincinnati, OH
www.matschca.com
sue@matschca.com

Dedication

Well, I have been told that I should write a dedication to this letter that has turned into a short book. As I sit here and try to decide to whom to dedicate it to, it dawns on me that I am indebted to a lot of people.

Dedication, huh – well let's see...first of all, my father, Donald E. Jones. I can see now that he, too, was bipolar. I can see now just how badly he suffered. I only wish that he had the knowledge I have. I really feel that if he did he would still be here today.

It is very clear that he, too, as a father, stayed alive for us. God, I miss him so much and that pain alone keeps me going every day.

My mother, brothers and sister have helped me both financially and emotionally.

My doctor, Dr. Winhusen, has helped me more than I think he will ever know. While he is not a psychiatrist, at least I don't think that he is, he has helped me get through this without being judgmental and/or invasive. Of all of the doctors that I have spoken with, he has been the easiest to talk to about how I am feeling. He has allowed me to come into his office when I am feeling down and out and I always seem to leave with a new outlook on my illness and what is happening to me. I want to thank him for being who he is and for allowing me to be who I am while in front of him. How do you repay someone for giving you new hope?

But I guess the biggest thank you that I have to offer is to my wife Lisa. It is amazing to me that she has kept me around for 20 years. If there were such a thing as a saint walking the earth she would win the prize. I have, through my illness and through just being me, given her one heartache after another. This illness has made me do things that I am not very proud of and yet she is always there for me. A thanks is not a strong enough word. "I love you" does not even come close to how I feel.

While I cannot predict the future and do not want to pretend that life is grand since I wrote my suicide letter, I think that I am safe in saying that Lisa will always be there for me. I can only hope that I can get healthy enough to be there for her.

Having three children is the one thing that has kept me alive. I never want them to know the sadness of being without their father even though I know that someday they will. I vow not to speed that day up by one more than is needed.

There are several friends that have been there for me. One that I must mention is Sue Veldkamp. Sue has been there for me and she has believed in all that I do.

She is my biggest fan when it comes to my music, my comedy and my writing. I want to thank you Sue for all that you have done. It is my hope that some day I will be able to repay you in some way.

For those who suffer from this illness or live with those who do, don't ever stop trying. Don't let this "thing" get the best of you. While I cannot say that it is easy, hell I don't know if it will ever get easy, I can say that it is worth fighting every day. You need to tell yourself that every day, 100 times a day.

Paul Jones

Forward

I first became interested in learning more about bipolar disorder after meeting Paul Jones, the author of this book, in September of 2000. Paul and I met purely by chance – he had sent an email asking me to listen to a song he had written titled, "Remember the Child." Little did I know that by responding to that email, I would discover a great friend and a man who has taught me so much about life – and what it means to live it.

One of the first things that Paul shared with me was the fact that he had recently been diagnosed with bipolar disorder. Being a Registered Nurse, I knew about the illness, but it was soon apparent that I needed to learn much more.

The first two years that I spent working with Paul, it seemed as if he never stopped. We always had "projects" in the works, but those projects were seldom completed. I often wondered if he ever even slept, as he always seemed to be "behind" his computer working on something. I was amazed at his "never-ending" energy. I could barely keep up with him.

As I started to compile information for a website I was creating simply as a "collection spot" for articles I had found doing research on bipolar disorder, I came across the "symptoms of mania" provided by the *Depression and Bipolar Support Alliance* (DBSA) and it was as if they were writing about Paul.

I was soon seeking out all the articles and websites that I could find about this illness. How could I begin to be a friend to Paul if I didn't try to understand what he was dealing with on a daily basis? I felt that I owed it to him to learn as much as possible about bipolar disorder.

Some of the statistics that I discovered during my search were shocking – the average time between onset of symptoms and correct diagnosis is 10 years or more – individuals who do not receive proper treatment for this illness have a suicide rate higher than 20%!

One of the most frightening aspects of this illness, especially for the friends, family and loved ones of bipolar sufferers is that many individuals with this illness resist seeking help.

As Paul will tell you, during the times he was manic, he felt, "great." He ha even stated that he was the, "best thing since sliced bread." So, why seek help when you feel on top of the world?

On the other hand, when Paul was depressed, he couldn't fathom that help was even possible – "so why bother?" He has described his feelings of depression as, "being locked in a closet for years, only to realize that the door was locked from the inside, but you couldn't find the key to turn the knob."

Paul was great at wearing a "mask" – hiding his illness from individuals around him. Instead, he would find other, more socially acceptable ways to talk about it. On stage as a Stand-Up Comedian, Paul would, at times, talk about all the pain he was in and the audience would laugh uproariously. He'll tell you now that it was his way of, "getting away with not having to pay for a psychiatrist."

It took several years before I witnessed Paul's "other side" – the horrific and all-consuming depressions that seemingly took over his life.

It was during one of these depressions that, "Dear World: A Suicide Letter" was written. What started out as Paul's suicide note - his "final words to the world" - has ended up being a vessel of hope and inspiration to all who have read it.

For medical professionals and those who work with individuals suffering from mental illness, "Dear World" offers a rare insight into the mind of someone suffering from depression that is also contemplating suicide.

Paul has taught and continues to teach me what true strength and determination is all about. His dedication to helping overcome the stigma associated with mental illness speaks to his true character.

After you read Paul's "suicide letter," I invite you to visit our website at www.bipolarbooks.com, where you can learn more about an illness that affects over 3% of the population. If you have someone in your family that you suspect may be suffering from or who is already diagnosed with bipolar disorder, you owe it to them to learn as much as you can.

I would like to leave you with what I think is a true definition of a friend:

"They stick with you and stand by you. They hold your hand. They watch you live and you watch them live and you learn from them. Your life is not the same without them."

I know that after reading Paul's words, which will follow this short introduction, you will come away with a new appreciation for your own life – and for those you "learn from."

I am proud to call Paul Jones a friend – and my life would not be the same without him in it.

Sue Veldkamp, R.N.

Dear World,

I know that you do not know me, nor do you probably care about what I am about to do, but before I leave this world I want to let you in on a few things. My name is Paul Jones and I have had all that I can take. Ending my life is the only way that I know that I can stop the pain that I live with each and every single day.

I want to share with you some of my thoughts and feelings on a few things before I go in the hope that it may stop some of the madness that is going on in this world. Perhaps it will shed a little light on life for those of you who choose to read this.

I am a 38-year-old man that has been diagnosed as severely bipolar (manic depressive). Now for those of you who do not know what this is, let me give you the definition that most books and doctors use for this disease.

Bipolar disorder (manic depressive illness) is a mood disorder, which means that the symptoms are disturbances or abnormalities of mood. Major depression is a more common illness, the symptoms of which are mainly those of "low" mood.

Bipolar disorder involves episodes of both serious mania and depression. The person's mood swings from excessively "high" and irritable, to sad and hopeless, and then back again, with periods of normal mood in-between. Different from normal mood states of happiness and sadness, symptoms of manic-depressive illness can be severe and life threatening.

However, because many artists, musicians and writers have suffered from bipolar illness, the effect of this illness has sometimes been trivialized and regarded in some way as beneficial for artistic creativity.

In fact, for those afflicted with the illness, it is extremely distressing and disruptive.

Bipolar disorder is the third most common mood disorder after major depression and dysthymic disorder. It affects about 2% of adults during their lifetime. Symptoms typically begin during adolescence or early adulthood, and continue to recur throughout life. Men and women are equally likely to develop this disabling illness.

The consequences of the illness can be devastating, and may include marital break-ups, unemployment, and alcohol and/or drug abuse. Bipolar illness is often complicated by co-occurring alcohol or substance abuse and without effective treatment, can lead to successful suicide in nearly 20% of all cases.

I guess that since I am about to become one of the 20% of these cases, here it goes. I have decided that if I am going to go, I am going to get a few things off of my chest first. I need to clear the air about some of the things that I have been going through over the past few years. I do not want it to be said, "I wonder what he was thinking?" This way, all of you will know exactly what I have been thinking.

You know, I find that being close to my time of death, it is easy to put life into perspective. I would like to think that what I am feeling and writing about are those things that anyone that is about to die would want to say. I wonder how many individuals die every day but yet never had a chance to say what they really wanted to say. I wonder how many people are dying today, right now, that have something to say that will never be heard by anyone else. I guess that is why I am sitting here writing this letter.

Violence

Where do I start? I guess there is no better place to start than with the violence in this world. A lot of people have asked me over the years, "When did all the violence start?" I have got news for you; it all pretty much started when Cain hit Abel in the head with a rock. It has been pretty much downhill ever since.

I cannot for the life of me figure this one out. Why is it that we feel as though we have to kill and hurt each other in this world? If you look back on the history of the world, you pretty much can see that it is one killing after another, one fight after another, and for what? What has any of this violence ever really done except to spawn new violence for revenge?

In my short 38 years, I have seen enough hate, anger and violence to last for 100 lifetimes. It makes no sense to me why we do this to ourselves. And I am the crazy one, right?

Now I know that people will find a reason for just about every war there has ever been. I know that you can say that if we did not have the Civil War then we would still have slavery in this country, but what I ask is this: "Why did we have slavery in the first place?" What in the hell would give any person the right to think that they can own another person? What in the heck goes on in the minds of people to think that they are better than the next person? That is what this was about anyway.

As I sit and watch the History Channel, all I see is war, war, and more war. I cannot see why we have to keep reliving these killings. Why do we subject ourselves to this type of thing day in and day out? Is this not the reason why we have become so damn numb to war and killing? Heck, we all sat and watched the Gulf War as though it was a sitcom. This war was brought to you by Coke!

When are we ever going to learn that killing each other is not the answer to anything? The only thing that war brings is more war. Nothing really does change. Look at Vietnam. The people living in that part of the world are no better off today than they were when that blood bath started. Yet we celebrate the death of our brave soldiers? It is nothing more than a crying shame that all of those people on both sides were killed and died a horrible death. For what? Not one damn thing, that's for what.

Even now as I sit here, we are watching the world decide on whether or not to start war on Iraq. For what? Our own President says that they have the biological and nuclear weapons of mass destruction. Who gives a rat's ass!

The answer to this problem is not to start killing, it is to try and get an appreciation for life so that these weapons are never, ever used. Don't you think that if we all tried a little harder to understand each other then we could get past the war and killing thing?

Now I know you may think that I am saying, "Can't we all just get along here?" and I guess that would be the message, but the fact of the matter is, is it really worth killing each other over? After all, you only live a short time, why spend that amount of time killing and fighting each other? The world is rather small and it is getting smaller if you think about it.

I often sit and watch the news and wonder what I could say if I were in the room with the leaders of the world. I wonder if I could do any better?

When it comes down to it, if I could talk to the President, I would tell him to settle his ass down and leave Iraq the heck alone. After all, if they want to use their weapons, they sure as hell won't think twice about it if we go over there and start killing their people.

Think about this Mr. President - if someone came on our land, what would we do? I'll tell you what we'd do; we'd nuke the crap out of them. What would that give us? Not one damn thing, that's what!

It is amazing what is going through my mind knowing that I will be dead soon. It is amazing what I can see now that I could not see before. Knowing that I am no longer in need of money, work, cars, houses or anything else that we say is important has made me see what is really important.

I wonder how many people sitting in a trench during these wars of the world have felt the same thing as I am feeling right now? God, I wish I could bottle this feeling. Why is it so damn important to us as a people to control the lives of other people? That's what war and violence is about, isn't it?

Control. Do we fight with each other simply because we want others to do and feel as we do and when they don't do what we want, we feel as though we have to kill them or wipe them off the face of the earth?

Is that what Hitler did? Damn straight! He decided that because the Jews did not do and see as he saw fit that his race was better. What does he do but simply try to get rid of a whole race. That's major bullshit and yet people to this day think that he was right. That's even more bullshit. We have people in this country today, Skin Heads that think that they are better than blacks, Jews or anyone else that is not like they are. The kicker on that is that we as a country protect them, saying that they have the right to free speech. You have got to be kidding me here. They have no right at all, speech or otherwise, to think for a minute that they are better than anyone else on this planet. Hate, hate, and hate, that is all this is.

Why do people think that they can infringe on the lives of other people?

I can see pictures of all the dead Jews in the camps and it makes me cry to think about what they went through simply because of who they were. My God, how can we do that to each other? This accomplished nothing at all. The only thing that came from it was more war and more death.

This type of mass destruction of lives is not just overseas though now, is it? I really want to tell Americans that we are just as much to blame for this type of thing. Look at the Indians. This has been a thorn in my side for a long time. We as Americans love to point the finger at other countries for the way that they treat people. We killed Indians for the sport of it. Our country was founded on violence and yet we sit in judgment every day. My God, we even have pictures of Presidents who did nothing about it on our money and then have the nerve to put, "In God

We Trust" on it. I would say, "In God We Trust, those Presidents that sat by and did nothing about it will burn in hell." I know if I get to heaven and they are there, you can send me straight to hell.

It just amazes me that we as a people can overlook these details and think for a minute that we are not guilty of the same, if not worse things. How dare we sit in judgment of any other country? If it were up to me, I would replace all of them with real people that we can trust that God is with. How about putting Martin Luther King on a bill or perhaps putting Mother Theresa on the hundred?

Of course, war is not the only form of violence that makes me sick. I think the biggest form of violence in this world that turns my stomach is violence against our children. How in the world can we hurt children? I have spent a lot of time over the past few years working with parents whose children have been murdered. How in the heck can this happen? One of the first things I am going to do when I get in to see God is ask him why this happens. I can tell you now what I think the answer is going to be. It is not God who does these things; it is the sick and twisted people of the world.

Can't we see that our children are the single best gift we can ever have? Yet not one day goes by when we are not killing them one way or another. How for the life of me a parent or anyone can kill his or her own children is beyond me.

When Susan Smith killed her two young sons, you would think that these horrible murders would have sent out a wake up call that we have a major problem in this world. What in the hell would make a mother put her children in a car, strap them in, and send them to their death in a lake? I want to cry just thinking about that. My heart hurts to this day thinking of those little children going into that water by their own mother. You can bet that the whole time they were gasping for breath they were screaming for their mommy to hold them and help them. You can bet that the whole time their lungs were filling up with water that they only wanted their mommy - the same mommy that just sent them to their death.

My God, how can that happen? What would make someone do that to his or her own children?

How about the lady in Texas that drowned all of her children and yet the husband and other people try to save her life? What in the hell is wrong with us? I cannot for the life of me get this at all. How dare we treat life like this, but yet we are able to cry when people die in the World Trade Center tragedy? How dare we cry for any of them when we kill on a daily basis? We kill and we let it keep on happening. We let people out of jail every day that have killed, only so that they can hit the street and do it again.

If I had one wish, it would be that when someone kills a child that this murderer is never allowed on the street again. Ever. Why do we not have a one strike and you're out rule here? Yet the lawyers keep getting richer and our children keep getting killed.

If I get anyone to think about anything from my own death it would be about the children. For God's sake, do something about them getting killed. There has to be something that can be done about this. You can no longer sit there and just let this happen. It has gone on way too damn long and it has to stop.

Abortion:

What the hell is this tragedy against children? Let me set it all straight right here and now. Abortion kills a baby.

Period. No matter how you look at it, it kills a baby. What in the heck are people thinking? This is not birth control! A condom is birth control, the pill is birth control, and not having sex is birth control. Abortion is murder no matter how you cut the mustard.

I am not a bible thumper but I will say this: you abort a baby and you are going straight to hell in a hand basket. If you do not want the child, then for crying out loud have the baby and let some one else adopt it. Killing the child is not the choice here. Not screwing is the choice you have.

If you are one of these holier than thou anti- birth control people, you need to realize you are dead wrong. The only way to stop the killing of these babies is to either stop the sex, which will never happen, or use all the money that you raise to get people to start using a condom.

I am so sick and tired of all the pro-choice and pro-life people I could throw up. Both sides of this issue make me sick to my stomach. I am glad that when I am gone I will no longer have to look at the bumper stickers on all the cars.

The solution to this problem is so damn simple it makes my head spin.

Another thing to think about is the fact that we in America let this issue direct the way we vote. We have people getting elected simply on the basis of how they feel about abortion. Tell me right now that this not the most screwed up way to cast a vote for someone. We don't care how they feel about anything else except where they stand on abortion. This is no way to cast a vote. Look at some of the Presidents and other leaders that we have had in this country over the years. Most people wouldn't let some of them eat at their dinner table, yet we let them run our country. This is amazing to me that we do this year in and year out. I know too many people that vote totally pro-life no matter who is running for office. This is pure craziness.

The bottom line is: stop killing children, period. Do everything that you can do to make the killing of all children, no matter what the age, stop.

Money:

Money is probably the root of all evil. This saying has become clearer to me as my life has gone on. If you ask someone that has a lot of money, they will say that money is not everything. Yet when it comes down to it, we as a people have placed a great deal in what it is that having money and/or not having money means.

There was a time when I, too, thought that money was everything. I placed a greater value on my own life when I made a lot of money. I am here to tell you right now that money means nothing when it comes down to it. It cannot make you a better person. How do I know this? When I had money, I was no better then than I am now. I know a lot of people that have a great deal of money and I would not let them in my house, no matter what. Your heart and your soul is what make you who you are.

Yes, we have to have money to live, but think of it this way instead. When you live simply for money, it does not mean that you are living, per say.

Now, I am not saying that all people with money are bad people. This is not true. What I am saying is that the people that do have money should try and do some kind of good with what they have. No, they do not have to give it all away - not at all. But what is the use of having it unless you try to help those truly in need of help?

I am not talking about the bum that is on the street simply looking for beer or drug money. What about your next-door neighbor that may be having hard times right now? Instead of feeling sorry for them, how about helping them out? By helping them out, I don't mean a loan; I mean really help them out.

There have been people that I know that are having a hard time and if I had the ability I would try to help as much as I could. It really does make you feel better knowing that when times get tough for a friend or someone that you know that you are able to help.

When it comes to money, do me a favor and try and teach your children that it is not everything. When our children see both parents working, trying to make huge house payments or to have fancy cars, we are teaching them that money is where it's at. I have tried to teach my children that whereas we have to have a certain amount of money to live, we don't have to sacrifice time together for money.

I urge the world to try and slow this process down with the children. Instead of living in a house that requires both the mother and the father to work, buy a house that will allow one parent to stay home. I know way too many people that work so much that their children are being raised by baby sitters and other children's parents.

I have a friend that told me that the reason he works so much is so he can buy his son the things that he never had as a child. Yet, by working so much, he never sees his child long enough to watch him use the things that he has bought for him.

I can tell you right now that the one thing a child wants is to see his father. Both my mother and father worked, and they worked a lot. I will tell you now that I would rather have been with them more than have things. Things really don't mean anything to a child unless they have the people that they love around them.

I would like to say that I am sorry to my own children for working as much as I did. I do want them to know that. Do me a favor world - be at home with your children. Tell them that you love them and hold them as much as you can. The money really does not mean anything to them without you by their side and in their life.

I think that one of the reasons that our children are so screwed up when they grow up is because they feel as though they have to live at the same standards as they were raised. What I mean by that is; if a child grows up in a wealthy household, they feel that this is the only way to live, so when they grow up and cannot make that type of money, they feel as though they are failures.

We have to stop giving children everything they want without letting them know where it is coming from. They need to know that in order to have these things, they need to work, and work hard for them. Working hard for things comes at a very high price and they need to know this.

Look at all the children that turn to selling drugs so that they can have things. Why do you think this is? I'll tell you why it is; it is because we as a people place too much value on things and not enough value on life itself.

When was the last time you heard of a drug dealer giving his money to a church to help the poor? Never. They use the money for things - things that they think make for a happy life.

In a nutshell, stop putting such a high value on money. It is not the meaning of life.

Entertainment:

As a person who has been in this business for a great deal of my life, I will say this. The entertainment world can take the blame for a lot of the problems in this country, if not the world.

I know that there are people who will think I am crazy on this one, but I am here to tell you that what we allow our children to see, do, and hear has a great effect on the way they think and act.

Look at all the school shootings. The kids that did them said they were acting out on a song or a show.

We as a people need to know here and now that violence, murder, drugs, and sex should not be used as entertainment.

When you allow your children to see and hear these things, it is going to have an effect on the way they view life. I have had people tell me that it has nothing to do with what children do, yet these same people have said to me that tobacco companies should not be allowed to advertise on TV and radio. How can this be? If TV has nothing to do with how children act on or what they do, then why not let tobacco companies advertise? The simple fact is that it does have an effect on children. Stop letting your children listen to crap music and stop letting them watch crap TV and going to crap movies.

I guarantee you this, you stop letting them watch and listen to this stuff and the entertainment business will stop making it. But you have to let them know why they should not watch and listen to this stuff. You have to teach them why a song about killing is wrong. It is wrong because it is. Be sure to show your children the pictures of the school shootings. Let them see the pain that is caused when these things happen. We have to stop protecting our children as much as we do. Let your children see the ugly things in life and perhaps they will try to do something to change it.

Over the years I have been around a lot of nasty, bad things and have tried to help. You can bet that my own children have been told and shown these things. My wife and I have let them be a part of it in the hopes that they will see why it is wrong.

I remember one time when my youngest was just a baby; someone broke into our house while I was downstairs feeding her. The baby and I were the only ones home at the time. I heard someone upstairs and ran out of the house through the basement door and went next door to call the police. I left the baby with the neighbor and went to wait for the police.

The person had left the house in the middle of all this but the police went into the house to make sure no one was in the house. During the time that they were searching the house, my wife and son came home. When I told my wife what was going on, my son started crying. After it was all said and done, we were in the house and my son was still crying. He said that he was scared. I really did not know what to tell this 9-year-old little boy. But what I told him was this; I said, "Alex, I want you to remember how you feel right now. I want you never to forget how it feels when someone does something wrong to you. I want you to remember, because someday, if you ever think that you want to do something mean to someone, simply remember how you feel right now and you won't do it."

Now I am sure that you are wondering what this has to do with entertainment and this subject. The point is this; do not hide things from your children about why they are wrong. By protecting your children, you are only hurting them in the long run. When a song is about killing, show them a story about a real murder and tell them why it is wrong for them to purchase that album.

The entertainment business knows what they are doing. They are making big money off of your children by doing it and they don't care about your kids.

Racism:

Being from Cincinnati, Ohio, this has become more and more of an issue for me over the past few years. Now I will say that as a kid I was probably prejudiced for one reason or another. I guess I can say that I really didn't know why I was other than that was how my friends were. I guess the reality is that we felt ill towards black people and other people of color because we did not know any better.

As I sit here and my life is close to an end I can say that when it comes down to it, prejudice is simply ignorance. Most people will not take the time to understand that all people are different in one way or another. This difference is what makes the whole world the wonderful place that it could be if given the chance.

I think that people need to understand that if everyone were the same, it would be a pretty boring place. I will say this though; the cure is not going to be easy because of the amount of ignorant people in the world.

I think that the people that can best promote the change of racism are parents. It has to start in the home. If you are a parent that points out or says mean things about, let's say, black people, then you can bet that your children are going to grow up to do the same thing. You have to understand that your children look at you for guidance and if they are learning hate from you, then they are only going to teach hate to their children as well.

Our politicians need to help out here as well. They need to step up to the plate more than they do. I have a theory on politicians and racism. I believe that they, the politicians, like it when we do not get along. It keeps us focused on other issues instead of watching what they are really doing.

You know, people that hate other people because of the color of their skin are just about the dumbest people on the face of this planet. It has caused more wars and caused countless numbers of murders throughout the whole world.

I would like to say this to black people; you need to stop complaining and crying about slavery. There is not one person that is living today that had anything to do with slavery, and quite frankly, white people are getting real tired of listening to it. You may not like what I am saying here, but since I'll be dead soon, I really don't care what you think.

It seems that every time something goes wrong in the black community, someone screams racism or blames it on slavery. You have to stop doing this.

A prime example would be the riots in Cincinnati when a white officer shot and killed a young black male. The black community screamed racism and set the city on fire. They stole stuff that was not theirs, they hurt innocent people, and they said it was all in the name of justice. What kind of justice was served in all of those actions? None!

The cold hard facts of this case are these: the police officer told the young man to stop. Instead of listening to the officer, he ran and was shot during the chase. Had that young man not run, he would not be dead today. This is fact. His mother stated in an interview that she had instructed her children to run from the police if they should ever be confronted. Now, in my opinion, she is the one that stuck the bullet in her child.

I can only hope that the world will some day see that hating another simply because of color or actions from the past can only spawn more hate.

Drugs and Alcohol:

God, where do I start here?
My father was an alcoholic. His father was an alcoholic, and probably his father before him. Now I must say that I have never had anyone that I know of in my family that had an illegal drug problem, but I think alcoholism is pretty damn close to the same thing and it makes no difference to your children.

My father may as well have been addicted to drugs. As far as I was concerned, he was. Now don't get me wrong. My father was a great man and not a very typical alcoholic. He never missed work because of drinking. He was never abusive to any of us or to our mother, but he really didn't care to do anything when he was off from work unless it involved alcohol.

As I have grown up now and have become more educated with my bipolar disease, I can see that he was bipolar as well, and this is probably how he dealt with it.

Now many may wonder if I, too, am an alcoholic. I believe that I am if I allow myself to give in to this disease. I know that when I drink, I drink to excess. This is why I try to stay as far away from it as I can. I do not go to bars any more. I do not keep alcohol in the house, and I try to stay clear of events that involve alcohol.

Now it may be that I do all of these things because I am afraid of becoming a drunk per say, or I like to think that I stay away from it because I know that it would be easy for me to just stay drunk instead of facing the life that this disease has dealt me. I cannot find it within myself though to subject my children to seeing their father drunk all the time.

I remember when I was a small child watching the adults in my life that I loved get drunk and then act the way that they did. If I could say one thing on this subject to parents that drink too much, it would be, "Please don't do that in front of your children." No matter what you think, it hurts them to see that. Think back when you were a child. How did you feel when some drunk, older person would pinch your cheeks or ask you questions in your face when their breath smelled of alcohol? It was no fun then, and it is no fun to your own children now.

I believe that parents are the single biggest reason that their children drink. I know that I drank because I thought it was the cool thing to do. Heck, my parents drank like fish, why shouldn't I? After all, my parents must be doing it because it's okay, right? So, why shouldn't I do it? And heck, they drank a lot and passed out. I guess it should be okay for me to do the same.

You see that is what a child is going to think, no matter how many times you tell them that they shouldn't drink. As long as you do, they will follow in your footsteps.

I remember as a child my father or grandfather would take my little 8-year-old body to local bars. I do not have to tell you how they smelled. I do not have to tell you who was in these places. What I do have to tell you is how they made me feel. They made me feel like shit, that's how they made me feel.

Old, drunk farts with bad breath and nasty teeth, patting me on the head and giving me quarters for the vending machines. They all felt compelled to tell me how much I was like my father. I can tell you right now that if this was what it took for me to be like my father, I did not want any part of it at the time. Heck, my one grandfather felt as though it was a good idea for me to have a glass of wine before going to bed when I slept over at his house. Now, how in the hell is a child supposed to look at alcohol when that goes on? Some may say that that was then and this is now. Times are different, right? I am here to tell you that I have friends that, to this day will take their children to our local bar after a softball game and drink like fish. They see nothing wrong with this at all. There is something wrong with it and I say that it has to stop.

Another thing the world needs to look at is how the beer companies have taken over advertising in most major sporting events. What are we telling our children here? I'll tell you what we are telling them. We are telling them that it is not only okay to drink and drink a lot, but we are telling them that it is cool. You see, our children look up to these sports people as though they are Gods.

I am begging the world to try and get away from the need for and/or desire for alcohol. I believe once you get rid of that, you will also see a major decline in the amount of drugs that are used in this country. It has to start someplace, and believe it or not, it starts with the parents and will work its way down to the children.

Religion:

You know, they say that there is no such thing as an atheist on death row, and I really do believe that. Religion is a very touchy subject in this country and around the world for that matter. It seems to me that everyone in the world thinks that his or her religion is the right one and that everyone else is wrong. This is one of the biggest problems in the world today. I think that this subject is the cause of most wars because it drives the way a society lives.

In our own country you see this battle every day - from taking religion out of schools to the most recent taking of, "One nation under God" out of the Pledge of Allegiance.

One of the biggest reasons that we have such a decline in the moral fiber of our children is the fact that they are no longer taught to believe in God. The fact of the matter is that if you do not have a belief in God or the fear of a God, then what reason does anyone have to do the right things in life?

If you look and watch the TV shows that show death row inmates, you will see how, that only now, during the hour of their death, do they reach out to God for forgiveness for what they have done. I cannot help but think that many of the crimes that have happened in this country would not have taken place if we as a society had taught our children to respect God a little more. It is reflective in our TV shows. It is reflective in the movies that are made, and it is reflective in the music that is produced in this country.

I can tell you now that my children go to a catholic school where they are taught to respect, and yes, to fear God. This has made them the good children that they are today. They know that they will be held accountable for the actions and decisions that they make throughout their lives.

I know that as I take my own life that I will have to pay the piper for what I am about to do. I know that I will have to answer to my God for my actions.

When prayer was taken out of school that was a major downfall in the school system. Children should have the right to pray to God. They should have the right to learn about religion.

Now I hope that you have noticed that I have not pointed out any specific religion here, and I have not done so for a reason. I don't care what religion you are, but you should have the right to believe and be taught about respect, and respect starts with religion. It is the very basis of the lessons of respect.

Again, I am not a bible thumper by any stretch of the imagination, but I will tell you right now that having some knowledge of the bible has helped me through a lot in life. I am not saying that I have not made mistakes, but I will say that before I have made them I knew that I was going to have to pay a higher price some day for my actions. Just as I know that when I end my own life, I will have to pay a price for that as well.

I have heard the stories of the child about to be shot in school and the last thing that they do is pray to God. So much for prayer being out of the schools, huh?

I guess the point that I am trying to make here is that we need to get back to teaching our children, heck teaching ourselves, to respect God - the God of your choice. I am sure that the words, "God of your choice" will not sit well with some, but I am not going to sit here and tell people that my God is the best

God. I have a relationship with my God that helps me through my life. I know that it may seem as though I am a hypocrite in the worst way being as I am about to end my life, and yet say that I have a relationship with my God. But the pain that I am in every day with my disease has gotten so bad that I can no longer bear it. It has become so bad that I am willing to pay the piper for my actions. I do believe that God has made me this way for a reason. Heck, one of the reasons may be that He knew that I would write this letter. I don't know what the reason is, and perhaps I will learn the reason some day. But for now, I simply cannot make it through another day with this pain.

I do want to share one observation that I have made over the past year or so. In the Catholic Church, right before you take communion, they have the congregation share the peace with each other. Now this is a time where you look to the people around you and tell them, "Peace be with you."

I have noticed that when this takes place, the whole church seems to fill with happiness. It is the strangest thing. Prior to this part of the mass, you can look around the church and see the pain on people's faces. Yet during this ritual, people seem to light up with joy and happiness.

There has to be a reason for this. We need to try and get to that point on a daily basis.

I suggest that every day you try and wish people peace and or tell people, "God Bless You." It is amazing what this will do for your mood.

We have to get to the point where religion is back in our lives. We have to get to the point where we believe that the things that we do, right or wrong, will not go unanswered.

Our children need to know that the things they do today will stand in judgment someday. Without any fear of being held accountable, you have nothing to lose no matter what you do. I think this is the main reason people do many of the things that they do in life.

Think of it like this: If a parent allows their child to do whatever he or she wants to do without any fear of punishment, what do you end up with? A brat for one, and for another, a child that has no respect for anyone or anything in life. God has to be looked at as everyone's parent on earth, and God is not a bad parent. He will hold you accountable for your actions, both good and bad.

It is too easy to do the wrong thing in life if you feel as though you are not going to be held accountable somewhere down the line. I would venture to say that many of the people, if not all of the people that are in jail, had no fear of

God at all. Yet, when placed in jail, all of a sudden they "find" God.

Have you ever noticed that they always say that they have found God and that they are ready to do the right things? To me this is a little funny because last time I checked it was not God that was lost, it is we who are the lost ones. We do not find God - we allow ourselves to accept the fact that there is a God because it is during the tough times that we have time to reflect on the right things in life.

We are finally being held accountable for what we have done and we can see now that God is there.

He does not cause us to be bad, yet He is there to help us every day to do the right things.

I know that what I am about to do is not the right thing.   I have thought about it and thought about it. God does not want me to do this, but the pain is too bad for me to get through another day of this hell. Knowing this, I realize that I am going to have to pay for what I am about to do.

I am begging the world to please put God back in the picture. If you do this, many of the things that happen that are bad will not be allowed to take place. I know that if we as parents put God back in the lives of our children, we will see a big difference in the way they act. We will see them become good people with good and kind hearts.

I am not saying that you have to go to church every Sunday and be able to recite the bible from front to back. What I am saying is to help your children have a relationship with God. Teach them that the things that they do during life will be judged some day and not only you but also God will hold them accountable.

Justice:

I guess there is no better time to talk about this than now. One of the things that this country, or the world for that matter needs to face is the word, "justice". Let's look at our own country for this subject.

We have no justice system in this country. I am not sure if we ever really did. You know, this subject goes hand in hand with religion as far as I am concerned. The word "accountable" is what comes to my mind when I think about our justice system.

Do we really have a justice system anymore? I am not sure that I can say we do. When I look at all the crime and the punishment that is given, it makes me laugh. What we have in this country is a bunch of lawyers in power that are only out to do one thing, and that one thing is to make money. We also have way too many liberal organizations that have no souls at all. They do not care if a child is murdered. They do not care if you or I are robbed. What they do care about is themselves and their agenda, whatever that may be.

Just as religion holds people accountable, we as a society must hold criminals accountable for what they do. The single biggest atrocity as far as I am concerned is crimes against our children; pornography, murder, and rape to name a few. Why do we as a society allow the people that have committed these crimes to ever walk on the streets again?

Now I do not want to get in to a big death penalty debate here. But I will tell you that I believe that anyone that does these things to children should be put to death immediately.

Anyone that hurts a child in this way has no reason to be on this earth ever again.

I know that there are people who will think that this is way too harsh, but I will ask this of them right now; "If someone kills or rapes one of your children, what would you do?"

If you are able to say that you would not want them put to death, then I say when they get out of jail, and chances are they will, they should have to come live with you for a few years. I think then you would change your mind. The people who do these crimes have no value to society at all.

I have often thought that it would be a good idea to make the lawyers that get a child killer off on a technicality have that same killer baby-sit his or her own children for a month. I wonder then if perhaps they would think twice about taking the case? This would make these lawyers a little more morally accountable. In my opinion, lawyers are at the bottom of the food chain. Now, don't get me wrong. Not all lawyers are, but the vast majority of lawyers are nothing more than money hungry, immoral people. You cannot tell me that in many cases these lawyers know that their clients have done some of these horrible crimes, and yet they will fight and fight to find a way to get them back on the streets. I say that if they are successful then they should have to be held accountable for their actions.

If they get a murderer off on a technicality and that person kills again, the lawyer should be held liable for the actions of that killer. Once again, this will make them think twice before getting that murderer off, wouldn't it?

I look at recent cases where children have been murdered and want to throw up thinking about what will happen.

I have been blessed in my association with The Nicole Parker Foundation for the past couple of years. Nicole Parker, an 8-year-old Tarzana, California girl, disappeared on November 20, 1993 while playing with a softball and mitt outside her father's Woodland Hills apartment.

Her body was discovered stuffed in a suitcase in the bedroom closet of a neighbor's apartment across the courtyard. Nicole's killer, age 23, was found guilty of sexually molesting and murdering Nicole and was sentenced to death by a Van Nuys Jury. He now awaits his sentence at San Quentin Prison.

There are still people trying to get this killer out of jail on a technicality. How in the world can this be? How can we even let him keep breathing the same air that this little girl did? I hope you all really read and understand what happened to little Nicole. This murderer stuffed her in a suitcase. Her body was found in his apartment for crying out loud and yet someone is trying to get him out of jail. Can't the world see that this is wrong? Dead wrong. How can any lawyer in his or her right mind want to get this person out of having to pay the price for what he has done to an innocent 8-year-old girl?

I am blessed with being able to do work for this family and the foundation that they started in Nicole's name. It has taught me so much and for that I am thankful. To meet the parents, family and friends of this little girl and to see what they are trying to do to help other children is nothing short of amazing. Yet you can see that the pain that they have still is and always will be there. This pain is compounded by the thoughts of people trying to get the piece of shit that killed their little girl out of jail.

Once again, their little girl was murdered and stuffed in a suitcase. Do me a huge favor - get a picture of one of your children and put it in your hand. If you don't have children, get a picture of a child in your family. Place that picture in your hand and look at it. Really look at that picture. Now, think about that little person being murdered. Try to imagine the pain that this little person is feeling as he or she is beaten, stabbed or choked to death. Try and hear their screams for their mommy to help. Think about them pleading with the person that is hurting them to please stop. Think about how they feel as someone is taking their little life away from them. Try to visualize the picture of that man stuffing their little, lifeless body in a suitcase.

Now, think about what should be done with the monster that has done this to the child in your hand. The only justice for that person is to have his life taken away so that he can never do this again. If you have the thought of trying to get this person out of jail, then I am afraid I have to say that you, too, should have your life taken away because you, too, are a monster.

This is not rocket science here people. You have to have true justice in this world. Hell, we have people serving more time in jail for tax evasion and drug abuse than we do for killing someone. There is a problem with that.

You know, as I sit here and write, it is more and more apparent to me that the way we handle accountability is what is wrong with this world. It seems that we are quick to lay blame on the other person. It is never our own fault. It always has to be someone else that has caused us this pain.

In the case of Nicole, the lawyers will try and find a reason why the jury made a mistake. Let's forget that this man killed a little girl.

It is so hard for me when I am in a depressed mood to hear about these kinds of things. It is so hard to understand why this keeps going on in this world. Yet it does time and time again. I find myself crying when a child gets killed, as if that child were somehow my own. I cannot for the life of me figure out how the parents of these children can keep going on with life. How does Lori Parker get herself out of bed every day? How do her husband and their other children manage to keep going every day?

When I hear of someone being murdered, whether it is a child or an adult, I cannot help but wonder how their families continue through life. What is the driving force that keeps them going day in and day out?

I pray to God that somehow, someway the world will see the need for true justice. That is the only way that we will ever start to prevent these crimes.

Oh well, I think that I have touched about every subject that I care to talk about. You know, it really is amazing how easy it is to talk about these things when you know that your life is coming to an end. It is amazing how your perspective changes knowing that you are about to leave this world. The truth is so easy to come by knowing that today will be your last day on earth. No wonder there is no such thing as an atheist on death row. Truth is so very simple and yet so hard to come by during life.

I guess it is the time for me to say my final goodbyes to the people that are in my life. I know that as the tears roll down my face, I must tell the people that I love farewell.

To my dear brothers and sister:

I want you to know how much I love you all. I know that as children and into adulthood, we didn't get along all of the time. I guess when it comes down to it; no family's children get along all of the time. You need to know that there is nothing that you could have done to prevent what I am about to do.

To my oldest brother Ken: I want you to know that as far as big brothers go, you are tops in my book. I will tell you this right now though; you need to lighten up a little bit. I have watched you over the past few years become very uptight about life. Try not to take it so damn seriously. I know that the business is a big part of your life, but you need to know that money is not everything. You need to take better care of yourself and do things for you once in a while.

My opinion is that you care too much how people feel about you. Who gives a rat's ass what other people think of you Ken? You need to like who you are before anyone else is going to like you, anyway. You have a lot to give to other people, but you need to take care of yourself first.

I know that life has dealt you a couple of blows, but you need to be able to see that you can get through it. I am so proud of the way that you have come through the issue of your son getting his girlfriend pregnant. I am so proud that you stuck to your belief of them having the child. You were right when you said it was wrong for them to abort the baby. I am so glad that you are who you are and are helping out the way that you are.

I know of all the kids in the family, you will feel as though you could have stopped this, but I am here to say that you could not have.

I want you to know that I love you very much.

To my middle brother Frank: What can I say here to you but that I love you as well? I appreciate all of the support that you have given me over the years. I know that you tried to help me through this and I appreciate that. You need to know that you too, could have done nothing to prevent what I'm about to do. I want you to know that as a child and into my adult years, I have always looked up to you for who you are. It was so much fun watching you grow up. You were always and still are a free spirit. Don't ever lose that quality. You have always been able to make me laugh. You are a gifted person when it comes to being able to make people feel better. I think that is why people have always liked you.

I will say this to you as well; don't take life so damn serious. Try a little harder to love mom. I know that sometimes the two of you are like water and oil. Be sure to take good care of her, as she will not be here forever.

I am very lucky to have had you as a brother and love you very much.

To my little sister Sondra: I have watched you grow up from a little girl to the wonderful lady that you are today - from being daddy's little girl to a wonderful mother. I am so very proud of you for what you have done. Going back to school and getting your Master's Degree is the most wonderful thing in the world.

Just because you are a Psychologist, don't sit there and think that you should have done something. You know that there is nothing that you could have done for me. I remember when we were growing up how close we were. I am sorry that over the years I have drifted apart from you. I want you to know that I know you are going to help a lot of people as you have helped me. Believe it or not Sondra, you have helped me. I know it may not seem like it now, but you have.

You also need to try and live for yourself a little more. Your children are good, solid kids and now you can take the time for yourself. You have laid down a great foundation for them.

A little career advice from your brother here. Try and get involved with helping children. You are great with kids and they need all the help you can give them. They need to be taught that it is okay to be angry, sad or mad. They need to be taught how to handle their problems and that violence is not the answer. You are a person that will be able to do this. The children will listen to you.

I love you very much and am so glad for having had the time that I have had with you. It has been a true joy watching you grow.

To my mother: God I am so sorry for putting you through this. I know that this will probably be the hardest on you. You need to know that you have done nothing wrong. You did your very best bringing us up as children. This has nothing to do with how I was raised. I am sick, Mother. I cannot take this pain any longer. I wish that there was a way I could just be small again and you could take all of the hurt away like you did when I was a little guy.

I want to thank you for everything that you have done for me not only as a child but also as an adult. You were a great mother to us. You helped us all through the tough times while dad was drinking, and you helped keep us together as a family.

As far as being a grandmother goes, I have watched you with the children over the years and have to say that it is amazing the amount of joy you get from the kids. They love you very much. I know that I do not have to ask you to keep that up because I know that you will.

I want to thank you for always thinking about us kids first. I know that many times you put your own happiness aside in order to help and to be there for us. Please take some time for you now. Take the time to write the book that you have always thought about doing. I know that you will be able to help a lot of people with your story.

I am so proud to have had you as a mother. All of the good things that you have done over the course of your life are something that you need to be proud of.

You are indeed one of the leaders when it comes to businesswomen. I love to talk to people about you and what you have done with your life.

I want to thank you again for everything that you have done for all of us. I love you very, very much. Thanks for being my mother.

To my wife Lisa: I cannot believe for the life of me, or is it that I do not understand for the life of me what has made you stay with me for the past 19 years with all of the pain that I have put you through. I can see now that much of what I did or may have said was the result of this illness. I do want you to know though, that I cannot blame all of it on being sick. I wish that I could but I cannot.

I know that when we got married, people said that a 19-year-old and a 21-year-old had no business doing so. I will say that even with the way things are now that they were dead wrong. Whereas we may have had a little tougher time, I would not trade one day of it for the world. I feel as though you have helped raise me to a certain extent. You have seen me through some very tough times. You have always been there for me no matter what it is that I have done.

I am very lucky to have found you. Even though the last few years you have stood by me and tried to help me get through it, I wish that I could have been there for you when you needed me. It seems as though I just couldn't pull it off.

I want to thank you for being the person that you have always been and the person that you have become over the years. It seems as though no matter where we were financially, you were always okay with it. You stood by the many crazy decisions that I made during both my manic and depressed times. You were always there to tell me that it was going to be okay.

During the past six months or so I know that I have driven you away from me. I want to tell you right now it had nothing to do with you at all. I am just so tired of you going through all of this. I don't want you to see me like this any more. I know that you have said that you are here for me and that I should not tell you what you should see and go through, but it is still tough to know that I am making you cry.

I don't want you to have to go through any of this ever again.

I want to thank you for being a great wife and a loving mother to our children. I want you to know how proud you have made me by going back to school and following your dream. You are going to make a wonderful teacher and I know that you are going to make a lot of children into great, caring adults. When I see the way you interact with children it makes chills go up and down my spine. It is like a little piece of heaven to see someone care about others the way that you do.

I look at our own children and I thank God that you are their mother. They are such good and caring people because of you. You have taught them to care about not only others, but you have taught them to love who they are for who they are. Not many parents take the time that you have taken with our children. I'd like to think that if more parents were like you that this would be a great place to live in.

When I look into the eyes of our children I see you. You are there in the way they act, the way they speak, and the way they love, and yet they are their own people at the same time. You are one of the most unselfish people on the face of this earth. I am very lucky to have had you in my life.

I want you to know that I am very sorry for leaving you alone with the children. I want you to know that I wish I could get through this whole thing but I cannot. I know that you and the children are going to be okay. I know this because they have you and you have them.

The last 19 years of my life have been filled with many great memories. I want you to know how much it meant for you to be in the audience during my shows. I want you to know that I used to look out in the crowd and see you laughing. It still amazes me how you can still laugh at my show. I can't tell you how many times you were at my shows and I couldn't see you, but I would hear your laugh. That alone made me feel like I was the king of the world. You made me feel as though nothing could stop me from doing anything. No matter how the show was going, when I heard you laughing, everything was okay. I can still hear your laugh in my head, and it makes me smile from ear to ear.

I remember how you were always there no matter what time at night I would call you from the road. I remember times that I would go back to the hotel and be in a depressed state and you would make me feel better. I remember how I would go to bed in the hotel room and even though you were hundreds of miles away, I always felt safe knowing that I had you in my life. Lisa, you have been a great friend to me and I will always be thankful for having you.

I want to thank you for believing in my music the way you have over the years. You are one of the few people who truly understand what it is that I write about. I want to thank you for telling me when you thought that I was not writing my best. I want to thank you for coming to the clubs to listen to me sing the same songs over and over again and still being able to tell me I did a good job. I want you to know that when I sing, it lifts my heart to see you looking on. I look in your eyes while I sing and it seems like you are listening for the first time, every time.

I want to thank you for pushing me when times got tough for me. You never let me just lie down to die. You have always been able to make me get up and get back to work.

I do not want you to think that you did not do enough to help me get through this illness. You have done everything that you could have done. You have given me all the space that I needed to have. I want you to know how much it has meant to me knowing that you are there for me no matter what kind of day I have been having.

I know that I have told you that I was not sure if I was still in love with you and even with that said, you stayed by my side. Whereas I cannot sit here even today and explain why I can say this, I do love you for who you are and what you have done. I love you for being a friend to me above all else.

I am not sure what this illness has done to my heart. I don't know if for some reason because of it I am no longer able to be in love with someone or not. It feels as though it has beaten me down so much that not only do I not love myself but also I am unable to be in love with another person. You have told me many times that I need to love who I am before I will be able to love another person in that sense of the word. I can see now that you are right. I can see now that until I am able to love who I am, I will not be able to love you or anyone the way that I really should.

It seems like too many times in life we see married people drift apart the way that we have drifted. I think that society has a lot to do with this. You know in the world today we place so much value on things like cars and houses and we place such little value on the simple things such as being together that we tend to forget. I know that some of the best memories I have with you are those Friday nights in that little apartment of ours watching The Love Boat and eating pizza. I remember how we looked forward to just sitting on the couch watching that stupid show. Back then we thought that we had it so bad because we did not have enough money to do anything on Friday night except stay at home and watch TV. Looking back now, we never had it so good, really. We had everything that we needed - each other.

I think that if I could tell the world one thing about marriage, it would be to sit back and remember the early days as often as you can. It may not fix all of your problems but it will certainly put the current day's problems into perspective.

God, sitting here thinking about that stupid little apartment, I was just reminded of how you let me build that dog house for the Great Dane in the middle of the living room. That doghouse was almost the size of the whole room. That is another thing I love you for. No matter how goofy my idea was, you always let me do what I was thinking and I sure as hell don't know what I was thinking there.

You have been an incredible person for me to have in my life, Lisa. I love you very much. I really do.

To my children:

Of all the people and of all the words that I have written today, I believe that this is going to be the hardest part by far. Even now, I am starting to tear up just thinking about you kids. Alex and MacKenzie, I know you will be able to read this and I hope that you will read it to little Olivia.

The three of you are truly the sunshine of my life. I have watched you from the time you were born become great, loving, good-hearted little people.

Alex:

You are 13 years old now and you may find that the next few years are going to be the hardest on you. I want you to know that you are not going to be alone during this time. You need to rely on the guidance of your mother and of the rest of the family. Being a young man is not an easy thing to be. I know as I have been there.

I want you to know a few things though, and I am not preaching to you. I am simply telling you how it is. Every father, heck every parent tries to teach their children certain things and sure as I am standing here it is not until you grow older and have children of your own that you see that most, if not all of it, is true.

First of all, you need to always be true to who you are. Don't try to be someone that you are not. By doing this you will only set yourself up to be unhappy. Your mother and I have tried to teach you that it is way more important to be you than it is to try and be someone else. You are a great kid with a huge heart. Always follow what your heart tells you. It is rarely going to lead you down the wrong road.

You need to always remember that there is more to life than money and things. We have tried to show you this. Whereas you will need a certain amount of money to live, having a tin of money is not going to make you happy. The one thing that will make you happy is to be who you are.

Please remember to respect the people that you come in contact with. Surround yourself with people that are true to themselves and they will be true to you. Good friends Alex are very hard to find, and they are even harder to replace. Treat them as though they are golden because they are.

Your mother and I have tried to teach you that winning is not everything and that is very true. The only thing that I ask that you do is to try 110%, no matter what it is that you are doing. If you try your hardest to give your best, you will always be a winner in life. There is way more to life than winning and I don't care what anyone says. Whatever you decide to do in your life, simply try your best and give it all you have.

I want you to remember to respect the women in your life. As you grow older, you may watch your friends treat their girlfriends with no respect. Please don't let that happen in your life. You need to cherish the other person that you have in your life.

You know how I feel about drugs and alcohol. Do not let your friends tell you what you should and what you shouldn't do. If your friends try to get you to take drugs then they are not your friends.

The bottom line is that you need to always have respect for your life. Keep your spiritual side close at hand. God is there for you to talk to at all times. Never forget that.

I love you very much son. Never, ever think that I don't.

Mackenzie Lee:

At the age of 11 you are becoming an incredible young women - my first little girl whom I love so very much. I want you to remember as you grow up that your mother will always be there for you. Whether it is about boys or what you want to do with your life, she will be there to help guide you through it.

As with Alex, I want you to always remember to be true to who you are. Don't think that you have to follow the crowd because you do not. You must realize that as a girl, some people may act as though you are not as good as they are. This is not true. Look at the women that you have in your life. Look at your mother, your grandmothers, and your aunts to name a few. We have some pretty incredible women in our family and you are becoming one of them.

You are a very talented little girl with a wonderful imagination. Be sure to use the gifts that God has given you. Be sure that you use them to do some good in the world because that is why we are all here anyway.

Always remember to be kind and caring to your brother and sister. Try to always remember how much you guys love each other. It still amazes me how the three of you can still sit and play for hours together.

I want you to do one thing for me when it comes to boys. Be sure to respect yourself and your body. If you keep a high respect for yourself and for your body everything else should work out fine. I know that you and I have joked about going to college, finding a job, then getting married and having children, but I am here to tell you that this is the formula that you should take.

Do not get involved with any man that does not treat you with respect. Do not allow yourself to be with a man that will not treat you with dignity. Make sure that who ever you have a relationship with allows you to grow and become who you are. It is going to be very important for you to be who you are.

As always, remember - 110% no matter what you decide to do.

I love you very much. Always remember that.

My little Olivia:

I know that you are way too young to understand or read this, but I hope that when you get older that you will read this and understand. I want you to know that God blessed your mother and I with you. Your mother and I were told by doctors that we would not have any more children and yet here you are.

I believe in my heart of hearts that you were sent by God to shed some light on life for both your mother and I. My life changed so much when you came to me. I really believe that you are my father's soul. I remember when your mother and I brought you home from the hospital. I was holding you in my arms. You were about 3 days old. You lay in my arms with your eyes closed. I whispered to you, "You are my father's soul aren't you?" With that you opened your eyes and you smiled at me, then closed your eyes again. I waited a few minutes and asked again, "You're my father's soul, aren't you?" Again you opened your eyes and looked at me and smiled and then closed your eyes again.

With this I began to cry and called for your mother to come into the room. I again asked you, "You're my father's soul, aren't you?" and again you opened your eyes and smiled then closed your eyes and went back to sleep.

Olivia, you are my father's soul and for that I have been truly blessed. You will never know what a wonderful man your grandfather was, but I know in my heart that his soul is living within you and because of that you will be a wonderful person yourself.

I have watched you grow into a wonderful, little young lady. You are probably one of the most creative people I have ever seen. I can't tell you what joy I get watching you play for hours by yourself and never getting tired of it. I know that you are going to make a huge difference in the world as you have already done in the very short time that you have been here.

You once asked me if you would always be my little girl no matter how big you got and the answer is, "Yes, you will always be my little girl."

Just as with MacKenzie and Alex, remember to always have respect for who you are and what you do. Remember that God is there for you during not only the good times but also the bad times. You need to learn how to rely on your faith to get you through life. If you do this you will never really be alone.

Remember that your mommy will always be there for you no matter what kind of problem that you are having. You will be able to come to her and she will help you.

I just want you children to know that you need to always try your hardest to make a difference in this world. You need to always seek your purpose and when you feel as though you do not know which way to turn, always turn to God and he will help to guide you.

Please don't be one of those people who think that God is going to solve all of your problems, as He will not. But by talking to Him and believing in Him, He will help you make the right choices in your life. I have found that through talking to God I have been given the insight and strength to get through almost anything at all. I think that you will find that by allowing yourself to have a relationship with God you will see that there is not that much that you cannot do in life.

I have prayed and prayed that some how and in some way that God would make these depressions stop in my life. I have prayed and prayed that He would help me see that there is a light at the end of the tunnel.

I have to say that I feel so much better now after writing this letter. It is almost as if God has kept me writing for a reason. As I sit here with the pills to end my life within reach at any moment, God has, in a way only He can, given me new hope. I feel as though through the writing of this letter, He has shown me that perhaps all is not lost.

The pills seem to be further away than they were but a few moments ago. After all, what have I been talking about? Do I dare read the words that I have written? And if I do, what and how will I feel about them?

At the time that I started writing this letter, which somehow has seemed to turn into a small book of sorts, I thought that being bipolar was the single, worst thing that could ever happen to me.

Now, being bipolar seems to be not that much of an issue. Perhaps I should take the time to listen to what I say and what

I have said. Perhaps I should take a look at what I have done and at the work that I still want to do.

I certainly have conquered bigger problems than this in my life. God has helped me before. Why is it that I am so eager to give up on Him now? Why is it that I will let this disease break me when in fact I have never let anything break me like this before?

As I have gotten closer and closer to ending my life, I feel as though I have, in my own words, given myself all the more reason to try and start life anew.

I remember the days when I used to go to high schools and talk to students about life. I remember trying to get them to understand how important it is to be the best person that they can be. I remember looking at the faces of these children when I told them to go home and write their own obituaries.

I recall how their teachers came up to me and said, "Why would you tell them to write obituaries?" The answer was really simple, at least in my eyes it was. You see, I would tell the kids that you could measure what it was that a person had done in life by reading the obituary of that person when they died. A person that had left very little impact in the world or on those who knew him would simply have a few lines in the newspaper at best. You would be able to read when, where and how and that was about it.

But a person that has led a productive and happy life will have several lines, if not paragraphs, written about them. In some cases, there will even be a picture of that person.

I remember when my father died, we could have written a book about all the lives that he touched. As a matter of fact, it was not until my father died that I really knew who he was and that is a true shame.

I told the children to take a look at where they were headed and if they were to die today, what could be written about them? I told them to go home and think about what they were doing and what they have done and try and write as though they had left this earth.

At the time, I had a couple people tell me that I was crazy for asking children to do this, but as I have written this letter it seems to have done something for me as well. I've come to realize that life is not all that bad for me right now!

Sure, fighting with this illness is not something that I want to do and yes, it is hard to get out of bed sometimes, but looking at it from the perspective of having to write my own obituary puts a new light on it a little, now doesn't it?

Let's see if I can do what I've asked so many children to do - write my own obituary.

Paul Edward Jones, father of three beautiful children; Alexander Thomas, his first-born child, a child that was sent from God when he was told that he would not be able to have children of his own. Alex is a child that is entering his teenage years and will have to face all the normal, childhood problems without a father. A young man that will probably never really understand his father, he will never be able to talk with his dad about girls, sports or anything else that a boy talks to his father about.

Mackenzie Lee, his first-born daughter who is as beautiful as the day is long. A little girl who once wrote that her father is the person that she admires the most because he can do anything that he wants to do except deal with an illness.

A little girl who was coached by her father in soccer and would look to him on the sidelines for approval of her performance, smile when he smiled, and try harder when he would give her that special look.

Mackenzie is a little girl who would hang on his every word when they talked about the facts of life. A little girl who would write short stories and leave them on the kitchen table for him to read at night when he came home and rush into his bedroom in the morning to hear his critique of her latest work. A little girl whose beautiful blue eyes will never again stare at her father while he is writing his latest song about life and smile in wonderment when he puts a reference of her in the lyrics of that song.

Olivia Donneta, the little angel that was sent from God after six years of trying to have another child. The littlest of the family who would rush to her father's car when he pulled up for her special kiss, only to rub it off and give him that look of defiance.

Olivia is a little angel that came at a time when his mother needed an angel in her life as well. Olivia, being only four, will not be as lucky as the other children. She will probably be very lucky to have any memories at all of her father - his memory only to fade as the years pass. She may never really miss the fact that he won't be there to talk with her about boys, school and other life issues. She will not have the memories of a father coaching her from the sidelines and giving her the cheers of hope as she approaches the goal to score.

Olivia is a little girl who, like her sister, will have to be given away at her wedding by an uncle or close friend of the family. She will have to grow older on the memories of her big brother and big sister and will have to create a father from those.

Paul is also survived by his wife of 19 years, Lisa Mary, who stuck by his side during the good times and the bad. She was there for Paul during his struggles on the road as a Stand-Up Comic. She was there for him when he thought up the stupid new jokes that he would try on stage and would tell him, which ones to keep and which ones to get rid of.

Lisa is the mother of his three children who put her career on hold so that their children would be raised the way that they wanted them to be.

Lisa is the women who, when Paul's illness reached a point that he could no longer get out of bed in the morning, would come into the bedroom and kiss him on his cheek and ask him if he needed anything at all.

Lisa is the woman who would come to his shows and laugh the hardest, even though she had heard the show many times before - a laugh that could be heard above all in the crowd.

She will miss the times that Paul would stay up late into the night writing a new song and then rush into the bedroom to have her listen to his newest creation.

She will miss the long rides on his Harley to nowhere in particular. She will find herself lonely the night that she graduates from college. She will find herself lost in a world that the two of them created over the past 19 years.

She will cry herself to sleep at night, blaming herself for not being able to prevent Paul from taking his own life. She will find herself growing angry with Paul as time passes because he left her to raise the children, pay the bills and grow old alone.

He leaves behind two brothers and a sister who loved him very much. They supported his every effort and looked up to him because of his creativity and abilities. They, too, feel as though they could have done something more for him. They will remember the times that they told their friends about Paul's newest song or most recent joke. They will step in to try and help Lisa as much as they can, but they have families and problems of their own and cannot shoulder the burden forever.

They will remember the times that Paul would make them laugh when they were down and miss the fact that this will never happen again. They too will become angry with their sibling because he took the coward's way out by taking his own life.

They will have to be there for their mother who now sits and stares, wondering where she failed her fourth child, blaming herself day in and day out.

His mother, who gave birth to her fourth child July 9th, 1964, now will have to deal with the loss of yet another child. She will miss the talks that they had and will never fully understand why he did what he did. She will now live out her life knowing that a child that she raised was unable to deal with something as simple as an illness that can be treated by something as simple as medication. She will cry every time she looks in the eyes of his three children and see his face in each and every one of them.

She will cry as she now watches his wife try to hold the family together, yet their visits to grandma are fewer and fewer since she now has to work two jobs to make ends meet.

She, too, will especially miss the nights that he would come over with a CD of his latest song that spoke of life. She will miss the encouraging talks that she would have with him, telling him to hang in there and just keep writing.

Paul was the kind of person that enjoyed talking with children about life and tried to get them to reach for the stars. He was at his best when he could tell children never to give up and to always try their best no matter what they were doing. He loved to talk to them about God and about having a relationship with Him. He cherished the moments on the soccer field when the girls were losing the game by score, but yet they were winning his heart with effort. He would tell the children that no matter how bad things would get in life, if you would simply talk to God and speak to yourself about life, you would be able to get through anything.

He would read the newspaper and look at all the tragedy in the world and then write a song to try and help those who were going through pain and suffering. He would speak to the parents who had lost children or a loved one to murder and listen to their every word, only to find more meaning in his own life.

This man forgot all the things in life that he had. He somehow lost sight of all the things that surrounded him every day. He let a simple illness that can be handled by taking a few simple pills get the best of him. He gave no consideration to all the things listed above and selfishly took his own life because he just couldn't cope. He allowed the fear that others would "label" him to destroy the lives of those around him without any consideration for them whatsoever. He let one simple problem end a life that, for the most part, had more happiness in it if he would have simply opened his eyes a little wider at times.

This man turned his back on not only his family and friends, but he turned away from the one thing that really meant the most to him, God. He was fast to preach but slow to listen to his own simple words, "Talk to God and you will be shown the right direction."

Just when I thought that I couldn't be shown any more by the words I write, writing the last few paragraphs, and writing my own obituary has shown me yet again that I cannot allow this to get the best of me. I will keep trying the medication until I get the right mix. I will allow myself to be sad and not tell myself that it is bullshit. I will not allow myself to think that I should end my life because of the pain. I will no longer tell myself that this is not fair to my wife and children, as it is really not up to me to decide that. I need to listen to my own words and again find solace in talking with God and asking Him for the strength to find the courage and the reasons to keep going and to keep trying to find that right mix of medicine.

I promise myself that I will try my best to help others that have this illness get through it as I have done. Most of all, I promise myself that when I am down and the thoughts of suicide come into my head, that I will read this letter over and over again because I know that this is God's way of talking to me.

Dear World: I'm still here...............

Epilogue

Paul Edward Jones is a person living with Bipolar Disorder, but this illness does not define who he is. Paul is a very talented and gifted singer/songwriter. He is an awesomely funny Stand-Up Comedian. He is a very successful businessman. He is a devoted husband and father of three beautiful children. He is a person that feels deeply and profoundly. He is my friend.

Before September 13, 2000, I could tell you the basic facts about Bipolar Disorder from my experiences as a Registered Nurse.

Today, I continue to work side by side with Paul and I am proud to be blessed with his friendship – and with his insight into this crazy world of ours. My hope is that by reading Paul's heart-wrenching "Suicide Letter," you will come away with a renewed appreciation for your own life

– your family – and the friends you have been blessed with.

Paul, may God bless you always. I am eternally grateful that He brought you into my life, and I am so incredibly proud of your strength to live – your guts to educate others – your drive to overcome the stigma surrounding mental illness – and your determination not to let this illness get the "better" of you.

Please don't **ever** give up the fight to stay well.

Sue Veldkamp R.N.

Endorsement from Charlene Butolph Former Training Coordinator for the Developmentally Disabled

Society is full of deceptions, from magazines to television shows featuring healthy bodies, exercise, glamour, and financial successes. Society as a whole measures one's successes by their job title., what they drive, how they look, size of house, whom you know and label of clothes.

Society therefore tends to judge and believe what they cannot see. If it can't be seen, it does not exist, which in my humble opinion causes a shallow and fake view of the world in general.

Fifty-four million people suffer some form of disability. 73% of those people have no outward signs of their disability. The most common complaint is, "No one understands or even believes me!"

As one of those 54 million people that suffers multiple disabilities unseen to the naked eye, I was overwhelmed emotionally as I read, "Dear World: A Suicide Letter." Paul's ability to describe the darkness of his disability was so real and unedited as to how 54 million people in this country suffer each day.

I found his writing very compelling and painfully real, describing the daily battles and struggles as one lives every day when having a disability that is not only misunderstood by loved ones at times, but by society as a whole.

Along with the daily darkness that Paul has so openly described in his writings, the reader is able to grasp how surviving each day brings a multitude of feelings and decisions one makes each day while living in pain. He is able to show the impact of this darkness and how it impacts those we love around us and shows how we look at life with a truly unrestricted view.

He accurately is able to show the reader the true facts of pain, agony, and loss of one's self as well as the love, hope, and kindness that must be captured each day as one survives an "invisible disability."

Paul captures the simple, worldly issues one sees every day from a totally different perspective as the world complicates and compounds the solution under layers of rubble.

There is certain strength and endurance one gathers and faces daily as the disability conforms a person that was so surreal in Paul's writings.

It was an honor to read his writings from the view of a co-sufferer. I highly recommend that if you have anyone close to you suffering from any disability, read this book and approach it with a truly open mind. It will allow you to see what your loved one faces daily. It will honestly open a door that many face daily and show the inward impact of coming to terms with one's disability!

Endorsement from
Kathleen Spiering, R.N., C.N.N.P., M.S.N.

Recently I was privileged to read, "Dear World: A Suicide Letter" by Paul Jones. The document is easy to read and well written. It is an introspective glimpse into one man's world, a man who is contemplating suicide. It may serve others well to know the thoughts and share the feelings that drive a person to thoughts of suicide.

I commend Paul's bravery in sharing this intimate study.

Endorsement from Bruce Gerken
Ex-husband of two women with bipolar disorder

Wow! I found Paul's book to be a very illuminating read. I think it's a real world version of, "It's a Wonderful Life." Having met Paul, I'm glad he (and God) didn't let the pain win the internal battle he's been waging! Believe me when I say that the world is a much richer place due to Paul's active participation.

I agree with his views in many respects and wonder why it takes us, as human beings, so long – 40 years of living, to achieve this depth of life experience. In the end, the true richness in one's life is measured by how much we give and participate in enriching other people's lives and certainly not by the outward trappings of success that our "perverse" culture around us worships so much.

Viewed from that enlightened perspective, Paul Jones is, indeed, one of the richest men I've ever had the pleasure of meeting.

Thankfully I'll never fully understand the profound pain he's been through, but I do very much know the drill and still bear the scars. You see, over the past 16 years, I've been a bipolar "statistic" myself, twice, and the pain is tremendous. Although I don't have the condition myself, I've loved, married, and eventually divorced two special women who did. I did everything I could to make them happy, but eventually grew emotionally depleted by their self-imposed remoteness and the truth is that I loved them too much to keep watching them contributing to the self-destructive pain in their lives.

If you know of someone who is wrestling with this bipolar demon, have them read Paul's book before it's too late. It is a very real condition but you have a choice not to let the pain win. Paul didn't!

Endorsement from the Depression and Bipolar Support Alliance Cincinnati, Ohio Chapter

Paul, your message is so powerful because you have the fortitude to stand up in front of God and everybody and say, "Here I am. I have a mental illness. I'm struggling with it. I live with it. But by God it's not gonna get me." You demonstrate the kind of attitude that people need in order to get themselves on the road to recovery. It's therapy that they'll never get from a drug, a doctor, or a psychiatrist. You are a living testament to the power of the human spirit. You offer yourself as a role model and you do it with love, humor and compassion.

Endorsement from Kim Case, Ph.D.

I honestly feel that the students learned so much from seeing that a real person had this disorder. Many of them undoubtedly came to class thinking of mental illness as something that only strange, homeless, oddballs struggled with. Now they know that anyone they encounter on a daily basis could be dealing with bipolar disorder. And I believe the stigma attached to mental illness in general has decreased since this experience. Paul, thank you so much for extending yourself so openly to us and sharing your life. It makes all the difference.

Endorsement from Ann Bobonick, APRN, BC

As nursing students, Paul taught them how it feels to have a mental illness, how it impacts a life, and how it impacts a family. The science of nursing is to know about illnesses, know how to identify the symptoms, and know how to treat them. The art of nursing is to truly understand your patient's perspective and then engage in collaboration with the patient in order to achieve the healthiest state possible. I feel my students have experienced, through Paul, what it is like to experience a mental illness, in this case, bipolar disorder. This includes the severe depression, severe mania, and thoughts and plans of suicide. This experience of understanding, "the patient's perspective" can only benefit each of the many patients they will treat during their careers as nurses.

As college students, they benefited. Many mental illnesses, or even periods of decreased functioning, first appear in college students. We know that the majority of people with mental illness never seek treatment, resulting in lives that never truly experience the beauty of life. Paul's message made it okay to say, "I need help."

As citizens, we all need to know that mental illness is not a death sentence. Tremendous stigma can bring such shame, guilt, anger, and even unnecessary deaths.

Endorsement from Virginia Hedger, MSN, Ph.D.

I would recommend this book because it is a wonderful way to educate student nurses about the realities of living with a mental disorder. While many people can speak on the topic of having bipolar disorder, Paul actually has the disorder and can relate his struggles well and vividly.

The students can identify closely with him and many are moved to tears as he tells his story.

Endorsement from James E. Sergeant
Medical Ethics Instructor

To be with Paul Jones is to be in the presence of honesty. He brought students into the life of a bipolar person. I found his honesty and hope very helpful and inspiring. He puts a human face on a diagnosis. He puts a human face and name on hope.